Possessing the Land

Joanne Ellison

Copyright © 2017 by Joanne Ellison

Published by Drawing Near to God, Inc..
P.O. Box 1274
Mount Pleasant, SC 29465

All rights reserved. No part of this publication may be reproduced, distributed, or transmitted in any form or by any means, including photocopying, recording, or other electronic or mechanical methods, without the prior written consent of the publisher, except as provided for by USA copyright law.

ISBN: 9798364108746

TABLE OF CONTENTS

Examining Your Spiritual Journey	8
Strength And Courage	17
The Scarlet Cord	28
Crossing The Jordan	37
A Memorial	46
Bringing Down The Strongholds	56
Achan's Sin	66
From Deception To Victory	76
Conquering The Land	85
Dividing The Land	94
Cities Of Refuge	105
Spiritual Communities	115
Transitions	123
Faithfulness And Obedience	133
Whom Will You Serve?	141
Reviewing Our Spiritual Journey	151
Bibliography	161

EXAMINING YOUR SPIRITUAL JOURNEY
LESSON ONE
OVERVIEW OF JOSHUA

Meditation
Not that I have already obtained all this, or have already been made perfect, but I press on to take hold of that for which Christ Jesus took hold of me.
Philippians 3:12

Main Theme
Studying the book of Joshua provides an opportunity to gain insight into the importance of pressing on in our spiritual journey. This study will provide insight into what we need to do as we prepare for the journey of life, how we can press on in our journey, and guidance for us as we enter into our Promised Land.

Lesson Focus
Overview of *Joshua*.

I. Preparing for our Spiritual Journey
- Day One and Day Two
- Key Passage: *Jeremiah 6:16*

Read the Key Passage and write down how it applies to your life.

_____
_____
_____
_____

Key Box
As we begin our study of the book of Joshua, I want you to seriously consider preparing for your spiritual journey. Many times we have boarded a plane and taken off on a trip with little consideration of what it takes for that plane to fly. On the wall of an air museum, it says that there are four elements of flight: gravity, lift, drag, and power. These same four elements affect us in our spiritual journey. If it were not for

the force of gravity, we would never be able to complete our journey. God's Word provides the force of gravity for our lives in that it keeps us grounded. Lift is the element that enables the flight to take off. In our spiritual life, prayer provides our lift and the Holy Spirit provides our power. There is an element of drag in any flight caused by the size and shape of the plane, as well as the load. Many times in our lives, we have unnecessary baggage that can keep us from actually beginning our journey or hinder us as we move forward. Drag affects the ability of the other three elements to operate. Often the baggage in our lives that creates drag is our determination to do things our way instead of waiting on God. Too often, we let the past haunt us and the future scare us as we prepare to move forward in our spiritual journey. As we prepare for our spiritual journey, we need to make sure that all obstacles are removed that either stand in the way of our believing in Jesus as our Savior or in appropriating the promises of God to our lives.

What stood out to you as you read the Key Box?

_____
_____
_____
_____

Read the scriptures below. When answering the questions, reflect on the theme of this section: *Preparing for Our Spiritual Journey*. When you write your answers, ask yourself how this applies to your life or your life experiences.

Jeremiah 6:16
How does Jeremiah 6:16 apply to you as you examine your spiritual journey?

_____
_____
_____
_____

II Kings 6:8-18
What can II Kings 6:16-18 teach you as you prepare for your spiritual journey?

Isaiah 43:18
What advice does Isaiah 43:18 give you as you begin to examine your spiritual life and journey?

Hebrews 12:1
How does Hebrews 12:1 apply to you as you examine your own life?

What spiritual objectives do you hope to attain through studying Joshua?

Joanne Ellison

II. Pressing on in our Spiritual Journey

- Day Three and Day Four
- Key Passage: *Philippians 3:12-14*

Read the Key Passage and write down how it applies to your life.

_____

_____

_____

Key Box
God tells Joshua to lead the people across the Jordan River and to enter the Promised Land. Joshua had to "press on" to fulfill the covenant promise that God had made to the Israelites 400 years before. In order to be able to "press on," Joshua had to be attuned to God so He could lead him. As we look at some of the events in Joshua's life, we will see some principles that we can apply to our lives as we "press on." We will also see how God provides strength and courage as Joshua follows God's ways.

What stood out to you as you read the Key Box?

_____

_____

_____

Read the scriptures below. When answering the questions, reflect on the theme of this section: *Pressing on in our Spiritual Journey*. When you write your answers, ask yourself how this applies to your life or your life experiences.

Philippians 3:12-14
What do you think Paul means when he says, *I press on to take hold of that for which Christ Jesus took hold of me?*

_____

Exodus 33:11
What principle can we learn from Joshua in this verse that will impact our lives?

_____

Joshua 1:9
What assurance do we get to encourage us to "press on" in our spiritual journey?

_____

Exodus 17:9-13
What does this passage teach us about "pressing on?"

_____

III. Moving into the Promised Land
- Day Five and Day Six
- Key Passage: *Romans 4:20*

Read the Key Passage and write down how it applies to your life.

_____
_____
_____
_____

> **Key Box**
> As we have already noted, God tells Joshua to lead the Israelites across the Jordan River. They had to cross the Jordan in order to enter and live in the Promised Land. The Jordan River, for us, represents the obstacles we must cross to move into our Promised Land, our place of victory, peace, and rest in the Lord. As we study Joshua, I will be referring to a twofold meaning of the Promised Land:
> - As an unbeliever, crossing into the Promised Land represents our acceptance of Christ as our Savior and receiving the gift of eternal life.
> - As believers who have accepted Christ into our lives, crossing into the Promised Land is the process of receiving the promises of God in our lives.

What stood out to you as you read the Key Box?

_____
_____
_____

Read the scriptures below. When answering the questions, reflect on the theme of this section: *Moving into the Promised Land*. When you write your answers, ask yourself how this applies to your life or your life experiences.

Deuteronomy 11:8-21
What does this passage mean to you regarding possessing the Promised Land?

How can we relate claiming our inheritance (promise) in Christ to the passage in Deuteronomy?

Romans 4:20
Consider ways you have disobeyed God's Word and how that has affected your ability to receive God's promises.

Philippians 2:12-13
How are we called to work out our salvation?

What hope do we find in this passage that the Lord will lead us daily into the Promised Land?

Joanne Ellison

_____
_____
_____

Life Applications

- Pray that the Lord will guide you as you examine your spiritual life.
- Carefully consider where you are in your spiritual journey.
- Ask God to reveal all obstacles hindering your spiritual progress.
- Read and reflect on the Bible verses given in our lesson each week.

Prayer

Lord, help me to know you more clearly, help me to love you more dearly, and to follow You more nearly, day by day.

In Jesus' Name,
Amen

Notes

Joanne Ellison

STRENGTH AND COURAGE
LESSON TWO
JOSHUA 1

Meditation
Be strong and courageous. Do not be terrified; do not be discouraged, for the Lord your God will be with you wherever you go. Joshua 1:9

Main Theme
After the death of Moses, God instructed Joshua to get the people ready to cross the Jordan into the land that God had promised to give them. He promised Joshua that He would give him every place that he put his feet. He also promised Joshua that He would never forsake him, instructing him to be strong and courageous. Joshua trusted in God's promises and knew that he must step out in faith knowing that God would be faithful to His Word. God reminded him to obey His Word (the law) and that in so doing he would be successful wherever he went. As believers, we have the promise in God's Word that He will be with us wherever we go. The Lord encourages us to be strong as we walk by faith and not by sight, following God's leading and obeying His Word. God's Word to Joshua to not be terrified or discouraged applies to us today. Are you fearful of what He has called you to do or of circumstances in your life? Are you discouraged? Remember the Lord's words to Joshua: *Be strong and courageous. Do not be terrified; do not be discouraged, for the Lord your God will be with you wherever you go* (Joshua 1:9).

Lesson Focus
Read *Joshua 1*

I. God's Promises
- Day One and Day Two
- Key Passage: Psalm 119:140

Read the Key Passage and write down how it applies to your life.

_____

_____

_____

Joshua: Posessing the Land

Key Box
God promised Abram that his offspring would inherit the land. However, Abram had to obey by leaving his home, not knowing where he was going. God protected Abram's offspring, forming the nation of Israel and leading them throughout the centuries toward the fulfillment of His promise.

If Abram had not forged ahead in spite of his fears, he never might have left Ur. From the moment he took his first step of faith, God reassured him and his descendants that He would be with them every step of the way as they sought to be obedient.

Abram's step of faith was the first step towards the fulfillment of God's promise to him. Later, God asked Abraham, God's new name for Abram, to demonstrate his faith by being willing to sacrifice his son, Isaac. Abraham knew that God had promised to form the nation of Israel from his seed, Isaac. But once again, God was looking for Abraham's obedience, faith, and trust.

What stood out to you as you read the Key Box?

_____
_____
_____

Read the scriptures below. When answering the questions, reflect on the theme of this section: *God's Promises*. When you write your answers, ask yourself how this applies to your life or your life experiences.

Genesis 15
What was necessary for God to fulfill His promise to Abraham?

_____
_____
_____

11

What holds you back from stepping out in faith and obeying something the Lord has asked you to do?

Hebrews 11:8-9
How can the Lord help you deal with any resistance to obeying Him?

James 2:21-24
What does this passage teach us about our faith when we do something we believe that God has called us to do?

Psalm 119:140
Are you able to say with confidence that you believe God's promises and embrace Him?

Joshua: Posessing the Land

II. God's Faithfulness to Israel
- Day Three and Four
- Key Passage: Joshua 1:9

Read the Key Passage and write down how it applies to your life.

_____

_____

_____

Key Box
God has demonstrated His faithfulness throughout the ages. He promised to never forsake His people. The Israelites; however, often forsook God by worshiping graven images and idols and hardening their hearts to God. The Lord continually reminded the Israelites to turn from their wicked ways back to Him, but throughout their history, they were rebellious time and time again. How like the Israelites we are! We continue to worship Him with our lips but forsake His ways. We become self-absorbed or the world absorbs our time and devotion. The Lord continually calls us back to Himself reminding us that He will faithfully take us back.

What stood out to you as you read the Key Box?

_____

_____

_____

Read the scriptures below. When answering the questions, reflect on the theme of this section: *God's Faithfulness to Israel*. When you write your answers, ask yourself how this applies to your life or your life experiences.

Acts 13:17-19
What three things did Paul say that God did for Israel that indicate His

13

faithfulness to the people of Israel?

How are Paul's words encouraging for us today?

Deuteronomy 31:1-6, Joshua 1:5
What gives us the assurance that the Lord will go with us wherever we go?

How does the assurance that God will never forsake you help you in your spiritual journey?

Deuteronomy 7:17-24
What does Deuteronomy teach us about the Lord driving out our enemies, such as fear and insecurity, little by little?

III. Joshua's Faithful Response
- Day Five
- Key Passage: *Hebrews 11:8*

Read the Key Passage and write down how it applies to your life.

Key Box

The Lord promised Joshua that He would be faithful to him, just as He had been to Moses. But just as Moses had to be faithful to respond to God's call, so Joshua had to be obedient to follow the Lord's instructions. God told Joshua that He would give him every place where he set his feet. The scriptures show us that God holds true to His promises. We often have a responsibility to respond in obedience in order for His promises to be fulfilled in us.

The Lord promised the Israelites that if they obeyed His command to love the Lord our God, to walk in all His ways, and to hold fast to Him, He would send rain on their land and cause them to prosper (Deuteronomy 11:22).

God continues to look for faithful men and women to whom He can entrust His promises.

What stood out to you as you read the Key Box?

Read the scriptures below. When answering the questions, reflect on the theme of this section: *Joshua's Faithful Response*. When you write your answers, ask yourself how this applies to your life or your life experiences.

Joshua 1:1-10
What if Joshua had refused to trust God to enable him to take the Israelites across the Jordan into the Promised Land?

Hebrews 11:8
What enables Abraham to respond in obedience to God's promise to him?

Luke 11:28
What are we promised when we obey the Word of God?

Deuteronomy 11:13-25
What does the Lord promise in Deuteronomy?

When you have obeyed the Lord, what has been the fruit of your obedience?

IV. Our Response to Others
- Day Six
- Key Passage: *John 15:12*

Read the Key Passage and write down how it applies to your life.

> **Key Box**
> The three tribes (the Reubenites, Gadites, and the half-tribe of Manasseh) had to leave their place of rest east of the Jordan, which had already been given to them, in order to go and help the other tribes fight the enemy.
>
> Jesus tells us today that we are to love one another and to lay our lives down for one another. One way we can do that is to help others be victorious in their Christian walk, just as the tribes of Israel helped each other.

What stood out to you as you read the Key Box?

Read the scriptures below. When answering the questions, reflect on the theme of this section: *Our Response to Others.* When you write your answers, ask yourself how this applies to your life or your life experiences.

Joshua 1:12-15 and Galatians 6:9
What are some ways you can encourage someone who is struggling in his/her walk with the Lord?

Matthew 5:16
What does Matthew tell us will be the result when we help others?

John 15:12
What does Jesus teach us about our response to others?

Life Applications
- Pray that the Lord will help you trust Him and deliver you from your fears.
- Seek out ways that you can apply the scriptures that we study each week.
- Ask Him to give you the courage to step out in faith to obey Him.
- Seek out someone to encourage you and to keep you accountable in your spiritual walk.
- Encourage a fellow Christian who is struggling with some difficult situation by using the words that God spoke to Joshua: *Be strong and courageous. Do not be terrified; do not be discouraged, for the Lord your God will be with you wherever you go.*

Prayer
Heavenly Father,

Help me to walk in your will. Give me the strength and courage to follow your leading and to remember that you have promised to be with me always. Grant me the assurance to step out in faithful response to your Word.

In Jesus' Name,
Amen

Notes

Joshua: Posessing the Land

THE SCARLET CORD
LESSON THREE
JOSHUA 2

Meditation
They overcame him by the blood of the lamb and by the word of their testimony.
Revelation 12:11

Main Theme
God has a way of working through very ordinary and very unlikely people. God used Rahab, a prostitute, to protect the Israelite spies. Because she chose to believe in their God and follow their instructions, she was protected when the invasion took place. That God would use someone like her reveals that He was looking at her faith, not her sin. God will work through anyone who is available to Him.

Lesson Focus
Read *Joshua 2*

I. God's Workings Through Ordinary People
- Day One and Day Two
- Key Passage: I Samuel 16:1-7

Read the Key Passage and write down how it applies to your life.

_____
_____
_____
_____

Key Box
In I Samuel 16:1-7, we read that God looks at the heart, not the outward appearance. God is not a respecter of persons. David was the least likely of Jesse's sons to be selected to be king; however, God was looking at his heart.

Rahab was earnestly willing to help the Israelite spies because she recognized and acknowledged that their God was sovereign (Joshua

2:9-11). God saw her heart and He worked through her to protect and save Israel's spies. Rahab remained faithful to God's instruction given to her by the Israelite spies. Through her faithfulness, she and those in her household were saved. The Lord continues to search for those who have faithful hearts and are willing to be open to knowing and following His ways.

God often works through ordinary people. He especially gives power and grace to those who are willing to acknowledge their sins and their weaknesses. In II Corinthians 12:7-10, Paul describes his weakness as *a thorn in my flesh*.

What stood out to you as you read the Key Box?

Read the scriptures below. When answering the questions, reflect on the theme of this section: *God's Working Through Ordinary People*. When you write your answers, ask yourself how this applies to your life or your life experiences.

I Corinthians 1:27-31
Why do you think that God sometimes chooses the foolish things of the world to accomplish His purposes?

I John 1:9
If you question whether the Lord will use you because of something foolish you have done, what must you do to "clear the slate" with the Lord and restore fellowship with Him?

II Corinthians 12:7-10
As you examine your life, how are you able to see your weakness as an opportunity for the Lord to use you?

Matthew 1:5; Hebrews 11:31; James 2:21-26
How does the fact that Rahab, a prostitute who came to know the one true God and was used by God in the genealogy of Christ, encourage you in your walk of faith?

I Samuel 16:1-7
What does God look at when He chooses to work through ordinary people?

Joanne Ellison

II. A Role Model of Faith
- Day Three and Day Four
- Key Passage: Romans 1:12

Read the Key Passage and write down how it applies to your life.

_____

_____

_____

_____

Key Box
Throughout the scriptures, we learn about the lives of many men and women of faith. These individuals provide role models for us in our life of faith. Jehoshaphat, king of Judah, was such a man of faith. In addition to the examples that we have considered, we are provided with many other instructions regarding our faith.

What stood out to you as you read the Key Box?

_____

_____

_____

Read the scriptures below. When answering the questions, reflect on the theme of this section: *A Role Model of Faith*. When you write your answers, ask yourself how this applies to your life or your life experiences.

II Chronicles 20:20
In II Chronicles, what does Jehoshaphat tell the people will be the result of their faith?

_____

_____

_____

Joshua: Posessing the Land

Hebrews 11:1-6
Using this definition of faith in Hebrews as a guide, write your own definition of faith.

How are you exhibiting your faith in the circumstances of your life?

Romans 1:12 and 10:17
What are some other ways we can grow in our faith?

Romans 5:1-12
What are some of the effects that faith has on our spiritual lives?

III. God's Faithfulness to Cover Our Sins
- Day Five and Day Six
- Key Passage: I John 1:7

Read the Key Passage and write down how it applies to your life.

_____
_____
_____
_____

Key Box
The early church fathers viewed the scarlet cord as a symbol of Jesus' atonement (forgiveness for sins by the shed blood of Jesus Christ.) Throughout the scriptures, the importance of Jesus' atonement is presented in different ways. Jesus represents a Lamb of God in the story in Exodus where the blood of the lamb was put on the doorposts to save the Israelites' firstborn sons from certain death.

Jesus shed His blood so that we, too, could be saved from spiritual death by coming into a right relationship with His Father.

Today, you do not have to hang a scarlet cord outside your door like Rahab did to demonstrate her faith. Yet, it is important for each of us to recognize the importance of our atonement through Jesus' shed blood for us.

What stood out to you as you read the Key Box?

_____
_____
_____
_____

Read the scriptures below. When answering the questions, reflect on the theme of this section: *God's Faithfulness to Cover Our Sins*. When you write your answers, ask yourself how this applies to your life or your life experience.

Exodus 12:12-13
What did God tell the Israelites He would do to the Egyptian's

firstborn sons?

What did the blood represent on their doorposts?

Hebrews 9:16-22
What did the law require done to the tabernacle and everything used in its ceremonies?

What did this represent?

How does the writer of Hebrews equate the Old Testament cleansing of the temple with the cleansing blood of Christ?

John 1:29
What sin or obstacle keeps you from drawing near to God?

How can you apply this passage in John to your present life?

Life Applications
- Remember that God used Rahab, He can and will use you if you are willing.
- Determine to deal with anything that holds you back from having the faith that enables you to be used by God.
- Think of something that can be a "scarlet cord" in your life.
- Identify some ways that you can demonstrate your faith to others.

Prayer
Dear Lord,

Grant me the courage to step out in faith and allow you to work through me. I pray that you will increase my faith so that I will not fear sharing my faith with others. Help me to keep my eyes on you, knowing that you are always faithful.

Amen

Notes

CROSSING THE JORDAN
LESSON FOUR
JOSHUA 3

Meditation
Then you will know which way to go, since you have never been this way before.
Joshua 3:4

Main Theme
Once we recognize the sovereignty of God and give our life to Him, through Jesus Christ, He leads us through many changes. These times of transition will always be a part of our lives. However, we need not fear for the Lord's promises to go before us, leading us along the way and removing the obstacles and hindrances.

Lesson Focus
Read *Joshua 3*.

I. God's Instructions to His People
- Day One and Day Two
- Key Passage: Joshua 3:5

Read the Key Passage and write down how it applies to your life.

_____
_____
_____
_____

Key Box
As you study God's Word from the book of Joshua, discover the value of having a Christian friend whom you can trust. Having prayer partners is very valuable to each of us. We need the support, the caring, and the love of other believers. Let your prayer partner encourage you, pray with you, and keep you accountable as you strive to discover and obey God's will for you.

Joshua: Posessing the Land

> As you recognize God's instructions for you from spending time in His Word, share your joys, concerns, and challenges with your prayer partner and ask that person to pray for you daily. Discerning God's instructions for you today is just as important as it was for Joshua as he led the Israelites. Paying attention to God's Word on a regular basis is a vital part of our journey with the Holy Spirit.
>
> Remember that Joshua did not give orders to the troops to cross the Jordan until he had received his orders from God, his "Commander in Chief".

What stood out to you as you read the Key Box?

_____
_____
_____
_____

Read the scriptures below. When answering the questions, reflect on the theme of this section: *God's Instructions to His People*. When you write your answers, ask yourself how this applies to your life or your life experiences.

Joshua 1:7-8
What did God tell Joshua to do in order to be successful?

_____
_____
_____
_____

Psalm 119:9-35
How does hiding God's Word of instruction in our hearts protect us?

_____
_____

What instruction in God's Word are you disobeying or tempted to disobey?

Where has the Lord been directing your path in His Word in the last few weeks?

Hebrews 4:12
When has God's Word recently convicted you of a poor attitude?

II. A People in Transition
- Day Three and Day Four
- Key Passage: I John 4:18

Read the Key Passage and write down how it applies to your life.

Joshua: Posessing the Land

Key Box

In our personal lives, we enter or walk into different seasons of our lives, not necessarily brought on by an abrupt change, crisis, or a significant event in our lives. We simply take the next step and the transition is smooth. There are times; however, as the scripture indicates where we experience a "crossing over" to where we have not been before, a totally new experience. These are times when we become "*abar*," people who claim new territory and inherit promises brought on by radical change. Although change can be jolting and unexpected, God is with us as we follow Him.

As Christians, we continue to face crossover experiences journeying into places we have never been before. The Lord uses these times to stretch us and to change our character to be more like His.

What stood out to you as you read the Key Box?

Read the scriptures below. When answering the questions, reflect on the theme of this section: *A People in Transition*. When you write your answers, ask yourself how this applies to your life or your life experiences.

Jeremiah 6:16
What have been some "*abar*" times in your life?

How do you handle a "crossover" experience and the fear of the unknown that it brings?

Acts 9:1-22; Matthew 4:18-20
How did Paul and the disciples respond to the change demanded of them?

What is your worst fear during times of change?

Matthew 28:20b
What does God's Word have to say that helps us counteract that fear?

Romans 5:1-5
What do the scriptures teach us is the fruit of persevering through suffering and change?

III. God's Leading
- Day Five and Day Six
- Key Passage: Joshua 3:11

Read the Key Passage and write down how it applies to your life.

Key Box
The Israelites had to cross over the Jordan at flood tide. The river was swollen by the spring rains and melting snow from the Lebanon Mountains. During most of the year, the Jordan River was about 100 feet wide. However, during the spring flood season, the usually narrow river overflowed its banks and became a mile wide. The Israelites had no physical way to cross the Jordan. They needed the power of God to do what they were helpless to do. In the same way, God works in our lives today. God promises to go before us in times of transition, preparing the way for us and remaining with us each step of the way.

What stood out to you as you read the Key Box?

Read the scriptures below. When answering the questions, reflect on the theme of this section: *God's Leading*. When you write your answers, ask yourself how this applies to your life or your life experiences.

II Corinthians 12:9
According to scripture, what kind of vessel does God use to demonstrate His power?

Joshua 3:11
What does Joshua say went ahead of the people as they crossed the Jordan?

What do you think that means for us today?

Hebrews 9:1-5
According to Hebrews, what were the contents in the Ark of the Covenant?

What do you think these items represented?

Exodus 33:12-19; Joshua 3:14-17
As you cross over into an unknown territory, how does knowing that God's presence is going before you affect the way you handle change?

Life Applications
- Set a regular time each day to read God's Word.
- Take time each day for prayer.
- Share your concerns with your prayer partner.
- Ask God to go with you each step of the way.

Prayer

Lord,

Help me to obey your Word, follow your ways, and not fear times of transition. I choose to place my trust in you to lead me during times of change remembering that you will never forsake me.

In Jesus' Name,
Amen

Joanne Ellison

Notes

Joshua: Posessing the Land

A MEMORIAL
LESSON FIVE
JOSHUA 4

Meditation
...be careful that you do not forget the Lord, who brought you out of Egypt, out of the land of slavery. Deuteronomy 6:12

Main Theme
God has done mighty things for us since the beginning of time. As people of faith, we must remember all that He has done so that we can grow in our faith and pass our faith on to the next generation. Memory markers and repetition are two techniques that are used to improve our memory. Using these techniques, we can better fulfill our responsibility to personally remember God's faithfulness and to obey His Word, and to teach our children to do the same.

Lesson Focus
Read *Joshua 4*.

I. Remembering the Past
- Day One and Day Two
- Key Passage: Joshua 4:4-7

Read the Key Passage and write down how it applies to your life.

_____

_____

_____

_____

Key Box
Setting up memorial stones was a common Old Testament practice. Many times when a significant event occurred in the life of the people of Israel, they would use stones to mark the place where an event occurred.

Today, we use memory markers such as pictures, souvenirs, or gifts to remind us of special events that are especially meaningful. These memorials help us to remember God's blessings and encourage us to go forward in our journey of faith.

What stood out to you as you read the Key Box?

Read the scriptures below. When answering the questions, reflect on the theme of this section: *Remembering the Past*. When you write your answers, ask yourself how this applies to your life or your life experiences.

Genesis 29:10-22
Why did Jacob create a memorial of worship at Bethel?

Joshua 24:14-27
What purpose did the memorial stone serve for Joshua and the people?

I Samuel 7:10-12
Why did Samuel set a stone between Mizpah and Shen?

Joshua: Posessing the Land

Describe a time when you know the Lord did something significant in your life?

What are the reminders of that event that have helped you recall what happened?

Why is it important to remember what God has done for you in your journey of faith?

II. Fading Memories
- Day Three and Day Four
- Key Passage: Deuteronomy 4:9

Read the Key Passage and write down how it applies to your life.

Key Box

We read in Judges 2:8-15 that it only took one generation after the Israelites crossed the Jordan River for the people to forget what the Lord had done for them. It is no wonder that the Israelites were reminded over and over again of God's laws and His faithfulness. The ease with which the Israelites forgot God's faithfulness emphasizes the importance of combining the use of memorials and the continued application of God's Word.

We must face the fact that it is also easy for us to move away from God's precepts and from recognizing and remembering His faithfulness.

What stood out to you as you read the Key Box?

Read the scriptures below. When answering the questions, reflect on the theme of this section: *Fading Memories*. When you write your answers, ask yourself how this applies to your life or your life experiences.

Joshua 1:8
Why did Joshua tell God's people to obey the Commandments?

Deuteronomy 5
Why do we still need to live by the Ten Commandments which God told the Israelites to observe?

Deuteronomy 6
What are some of the reasons for obeying the Ten Commandments (v.3)?

What has been the result in our society of our disregard of the Ten Commandments?

What is the greatest commandment we are to follow (v. 5)?

I John 5:3
How do we show our love for God?

Deuteronomy 11:18-21
How can we both model and teach our children to grow in their faith?

III. Taking a Risk
- Day Five and Day Six
- Key Passage: Luke 9:24

Read the Key Passage and write down how it applies to your life.

Key Box
The Israelites had to take a risk when they stepped into the swollen waters of the Jordan River. Such a risk involves trusting God to go before us even when we do not see Him.

Wandering in the wilderness brought about the death of an entire generation of people. They were unwilling to surrender and trust God to take them into the Promised Land, which was to be a place of freedom. It was the next generation who chose to believe God's promise and obey. They were the ones who entered into the freedom and the new life that God had promised them.

Joshua: Posessing the Land

In the same way, before we actually take the risk of taking the first step in obeying what God wants us to do, we must be willing to trust God and make the decision to cross. Just as God went with the Israelites, He will go with us.

As the Israelites crossed the Jordan River and went into the Promised Land, they did it together. Today, we need Christian companions on our journey of faith to help and encourage us along the way. According to Warren Wiersbe, when Israel crossed the Jordan River, it was not the obedient arm of a leader that brought the miracle, but the obedient feet of the people.

What stood out to you as you read the Key Box?

_____
_____
_____
_____

Read the scriptures below. When answering the questions, reflect on the theme of this section: *Taking a Risk*. When you write your answers, ask yourself how this applies to your life or your life experiences.

Matthew 10:37-39; Luke 9:23-25
What habits, patterns of living, and ways of thinking do you need to surrender to God?

_____
_____
_____
_____

What keeps you from being willing to take the risk and surrender to God?

_____
_____

Joshua 3:6 – 4:11
Where was God's Presence as they crossed the Jordan?

How can disobedience be an obstacle to the Lord's leading in your life?

Describe a time in your journey of faith when you risked leaving a wilderness area in your life.

How did your wilderness experience relate to your obedience or lack of obedience of something the Lord had told you to do?

What was the fruit of your stepping out and taking a risk?

In your journey of faith, what are some things you can do to help you remember God's powerful faithfulness?

How do you think that passing these memories on to the next generation will build their faith as well?

Life Applications

- Consider the ways that the Lord has been faithful to you over the years and create memory markers to remind you of these events.
- Share your memory makers with a friend.
- Apply God's Word to your life on a daily basis to help you to remember Him in all you do and say.
- Make a decision to surrender to the Lord in any area of your life where you are struggling.
- Determine to be obedient to what God wants you to do.

Joanne Ellison

Prayer

Heavenly Father,

Thank You for Your faithfulness and goodness to me. Help me to recall all of Your promises in Your Word and to remember how often You have answered my prayers and heard the cry of my heart.

In Jesus' Name,
Amen

Notes

Joshua: Posessing the Land

BRINGING DOWN THE STRONGHOLDS
LESSON SIX
JOSHUA 5 & 6

Meditation
See, I have delivered Jericho into your hands, along with its king and its fighting men. Joshua 6:2

Main Theme
God wants to bring down the strongholds of our lives that cause defeat in our spiritual lives. He longs to be our stronghold and our safe refuge. A stronghold in our lives according to *II Corinthians 10:4-5* is anything that exalts itself above God, for example: relationships, job, ministry, or personal issues such as self-reliance, fear, insecurity, etc. "Jericho" represents these strongholds in our lives. The Lord: however, longs to be our stronghold and our safe place (Psalm 26:1-2). Webster defines a stronghold as a fortified place. We can build up walls of fortification that close out both the Lord and other people then these become our "Jericho". Entry into Jericho represented entry into the land that God had promised the Israelites. As believers, when we surrender our "fortified places" to the Lord and allow our "Jericho" to come down, we will be able to receive the promises in God's Word. What man-made defenses need to come down in your life so that the Lord can bring you to a place of freedom and promise?

Lesson Focus
Read *Joshua 5 and 6*.

I. Circumcising and Consecrating
- Day One and Day Two
- Key Passage: Ezekiel 36:26

Read the Key Passage and write down how it applies to your life.

_____

_____

_____

_____

49

Key Box
The Israelites who came out of the wilderness had not been circumcised. Circumcision marked every male as entering into a covenant relationship with God. Israel again had to be consecrated by the act of circumcision before taking possession of the land. For New Testament believers, the Holy Spirit in us marks us as God's covenant people. God gives us His Holy Spirit so that we can obey Him and enter into His service.

What stood out to you as you read the Key Box?

_____

_____

_____

_____

Read the scriptures below. When answering the questions, reflect on the theme of this section: *Circumcising and Consecrating*. When you write your answers, ask yourself how this applies to your life or your life experiences.

Ezekiel 36:26-27
What does Ezekiel say that helps you identify how you can control areas of difficulty and submit them to the Lord?

_____

_____

_____

_____

Genesis 17:10-11; Exodus 4:24-26
If circumcision identified the Israelites with their covenant relationship with God, then how does our willingness to "cut away" our self-rule and submit to God's control translate into our relationship with God?

_____

_____

Joshua: Posessing the Land

Once you have willingly allowed the Lord to cut away an area of "flesh" in your life, why do you think it is prudent to allow yourself to take some time to heal before moving ahead?

Since the Israelites' next step was to take down the city of Jericho, why do you think it was important for them to be circumcised first?

Ezekiel 11:19; Ezekiel 36:26-27
According to the reference in Ezekiel, why do you think it is important for us to have circumcised hearts before we enter into battle?

II. Removing the Reproach of Egypt
- Day Three and Day Four
- Key Passage: Joshua 5:9

Read the Key Passage and write down how it applies to your life.

51

> **Key Box**
> Wilderness Christians are often unable to display God's power because they are self-reliant, not God-reliant. When the Israelites left Egypt, the Egyptians saw God's power displayed as He brought about their release. For forty years, however, the Israelites lived in the desert lacking faith and power, complaining, and longing to return to Egypt. When the Israelites finally crossed the Jordan River, God once more displayed His power. The Amorite and Canaanite kings along the coast, who had been skeptical of the power of God, now saw God's power displayed as the Israelites crossed the Jordan River. Now the reproach (disgrace, discredit) was removed as the Israelites finally left the desert and moved into the Promised Land.

What stood out to you as you read the Key Box?

Read the scriptures below. When answering the questions, reflect on the theme of this section: *Removing the Reproach of Egypt.* When you write your answers, ask yourself how this applies to your life or your life experiences.

Exodus 32:1-14
Describe the behavior of the Israelites while in the wilderness.

Joshua: Posessing the Land

Why do you think that in our "wilderness times" it is tempting to fashion our own "gods"?

How did the Lord respond to the plea of Moses to spare the rebellious Israelites?

Deuteronomy 9:7-29

What argument did Moses use to cause God to relent and not destroy the Israelites?

If God had allowed the Israelites to die in the wilderness, how would that have impacted history?

By allowing the children of the rebellious Israelites to enter into the Promised Land, how did that enable the "reproach" of Egypt to be removed?

Joshua 5:1-10

What did God tell Joshua about the reproach of Egypt after the Israelites were circumcised?

Why do you think that the disgrace was removed?

In your personal life, what have you done that has given opportunity for the "reproach of Egypt"?

When have you seen the Lord remove the disgrace of sin and bondage in your life?

III. Pulling Down Strongholds
- Day Five and Day Six
- Key Passage: Joshua 5:13-14

Read the Key Passage and write down how it applies to your life.

Key Box
Joshua was near Jericho, perhaps contemplating a strategy to take down the stronghold of Jericho. According to the Scripture, he was a man with his sword drawn. Once the man identified himself, Joshua fell face down on the ground. At the point when Joshua recognized the Commander of the army of the Lord, Joshua relinquished his "good ideas" and strategies to take down Jericho and submitted to God's instruction (v. 14).

Although Joshua may have thought God's plan was a foolish way to conquer Jericho, he followed the Lord's instruction to march around the city for six days with all the armed men. On the seventh day, he was told to march around the city seven times. Then when the priests blew the trumpets, the people were told to shout and the walls of the city would fall down. God's plans may seem foolish or impossible according to our human reasoning, but His plans always work.

What stood out to you as you read the Key Box?

Read the scriptures below. When answering the questions, reflect on the theme of this section: *Pulling Down Strongholds*. When you write your answers, ask yourself how this applies to your life or your life experiences.

Joshua 5:13-15
When Joshua saw the man referred to in verse 13, why do you think he fell face down?

Psalm 27:1
When we consider the strongholds in our lives, what attitude should we have towards God?

Proverbs 3:5
How do we apply this verse when facing the strongholds of our lives?

Name any strongholds that hinder your relationship with God.

What would the result be in your life if you allowed God to pull down "enemy" strongholds?

Joshua 6:1-5
Why do you think that God asked Joshua to do something that seemed so futile?

II Samuel 22:31
How can obeying God's Word apply to your personal life?

Life Applications
- Commit your life anew to the Lord and surrender afresh to His plans.
- Pray and ask the Holy Spirit to reveal the strongholds in your life.
- Ask the Lord to do the work in you that you are powerless to do.
- Remember that God knows what is best for each of us.

Joanne Ellison

Prayer
Dear Lord,

Forgive me for building up walls that prevent me from loving You and others. I surrender the fortified places of my life and ask You to fill those places with Your love and goodness.

In Jesus' Name,
Amen

Notes

Joshua: Posessing the Land

ACHAN'S SIN
LESSON SEVEN
JOSHUA 7 & 8

Meditation
The Lord said to Joshua, "Get up! Why have you fallen on your face? Israel has sinned; they have transgressed my covenant that I commanded them; they have taken some of the devoted things; they have stolen and lied and put them among their own belongings. Therefore the people of Israel cannot stand before their enemies. They turn their backs before their enemies, because they have become devoted for destruction. I will be with you no more, unless you destroy the devoted things from among you. Joshua 7:10-12

Main Theme
All sin is against God and separates us from God who is our source of life. There are always consequences for our sin, but when we turn back to the Lord and turn away from our sin, He forgives and restores us back to fellowship with Him.

Lesson Focus
Read *Joshua 7 and 8*.

I. Sin's Consequences
- Day and Day Two
- Key Passage: Hebrews 12:1

Read the Key Passage and write down how it applies to your life.

_____
_____
_____
_____

Key Box
Sin affects each of us and it affects the people with whom we are in community.

Achan's greed prompted him to steal a robe and gold from Jericho.

> The consequences brought about defeat in the battle for Israel and ultimately his sin led to the death of his family and himself. Just as Achan's sin brought about defeat to the Israelites, the same is true of us today. The disobedience of one person can have a profound effect on a whole community. No person is a lone island because whatever we do touches lives whether for good or for evil. Divine justice demands full retribution for the wrong done.

What stood out to you as you read the Key Box?

Read the scriptures below. When answering the questions, reflect on the theme of this section: *Sin's Consequences*. When you write your answers, ask yourself how this applies to your life or your life experiences.

Joshua 7:1-12
What happened to the Israelites at Ai when they first tried to take over the city?

How did God regard Achan's sin (v. 11)?

Can you think of a time when you have sinned and others were affected by your sin?

Numbers 5:1-10
What were the Israelites required to do to make restitution or right the wrong both with God and with others?

In our world today, how do we see evidence of the sins of others affecting whole communities?

Romans 6:23
What are the wages of sin?

I John 1:9
As believers, when we sin, what must we do to receive forgiveness?

II. Disobedience and Forgiveness
- Day Three and Four
- Key Passage: II Chronicles 7:14

Read the Key Passage and write down how it applies to your life.

> **Key Box**
> Joshua sent men from Jericho to Ai to spy out the region. We see no mention that he consulted first with the Lord. The report came back not to worry all the people, to go and fight because there were only a few men in Ai and it could easily be taken. A small army was sent on the advice of the spies, and the men of Ai chased the Israelites from the city killing thirty-six Israeli men. Joshua, upon hearing the bad news, fell face down before the Lord.

What stood out to you as you read the Key Box?

Read the scriptures below. When answering the questions, reflect on the theme of this section: *Disobedience and Forgiveness*. When you write your answers, ask yourself how this applies to your life or your life experiences.

Joshua: Posessing the Land

Joshua 7:6-12

What was Joshua's attitude towards the Lord after the Israelites were first defeated at Ai?

What did the Lord tell Joshua was the reason for their defeat?

Why do you think that the Lord allows us to feel defeated when we have sinned?

What do you think could be a personal value in experiencing defeat?

How do you think the Lord's instructions to Joshua that the Israelites were not to take devoted things (booty) apply to us in our spiritual journey (v. 11)?

Acts 3:19
What does the Lord promise us when we turn to Him and ask for forgiveness?

III. Defeat Turned Into Victory
- Day Five and Day Six
- Key Passage: Romans 3:23-24

Read the Key Passage and write down how it applies to your life.

Key Box
We all have sinned. Our fallen nature causes us to continue to sin although like Paul we are frustrated by doing what we don't want to do (sin). Joshua searched for the cause of their defeat. Then, he dealt with the sin. After dealing with the sin, he moved forward to obey the Lord. As believers, when we turn and confess our sin and deal with it, the Lord gives us another chance just as He did Joshua (I John 1:9). His words to us, as they were to Joshua after the sin in the camp was dealt with, were: *Do not be afraid; do not be discouraged...* Joshua 8:1

Then, Joshua turned to the Lord for help. This time, he was willing

Joshua: Posessing the Land

> to do it God's way, even though he may have preferred to use a different military strategy. Again, the strategy was not one of a straightforward attack. The Lord gave specific instructions to Joshua for His military strategy on the city of Ai.

What stood out to you as you read the Key Box?

Read the scriptures below. When answering the questions, reflect on the theme of this section: *Defeat Turned Into Victory*. When you write your answers, ask yourself how this applies to your life or your life experiences.

Joshua 8
What happened the next time the Israelites attacked Ai?

How does Joshua's response to the Lord's instruction apply to us today?

What is the best way to keep from running ahead of the Lord or doing things your own way?

What do you think is the significance for us today of Joshua building an altar to the Lord after the successful attack on Ai?

Why did Joshua use "uncut" stones for the altar?

Proverbs 3:5
How do you keep from not relying on your own understanding and wisdom, and instead lean on God's wisdom?

Romans 7:1-14
What was Paul's struggle?

According to this same passage, how are we victorious against our sin?

I John 1:8-10
What does this passage say concerning our sin?

According to this passage, how do we obtain victory over our sins?

Life Applications
- Ask God to reveal any area of your life where you are "missing the mark" in what God would have you do.
- Recognize that God will turn it around for good if you are willing to walk according to His purposes.
- Follow the Lord's instructions even if they do not line up with your human reasoning.
- Pray with a prayer partner that God will help you line up any and all areas of your life according to God's will.

Prayer
Lord,

Forgive me for the sins that I have both willfully and unwillfully committed against You and others. Help me to see the areas of my life that are in conflict with Your Word. Lead me to freedom as I repent and turn away from my rebellion and sin.

In Jesus' Name,
Amen

Notes

Joshua: Posessing the Land

FROM DECEPTION TO VICTORY
LESSON EIGHT
JOSHUA 9

Meditation
*...for Satan himself masquerades as an angel of light*II Corinthians 11:14

Main Theme
Today we live in a world of deception. It is accepted as just a matter of fact. But, God did not mean for His children to live a life of deception. Everywhere we turn we are faced with attempts to deceive us, but God is able to give us the victory from living a life of deception. God can help us to be alert to Satan's deceptive practices when we depend on Him and walk in His ways.

Lesson Focus
Read *Joshua 9*.

I. Satan, the Father of Lies
- Day One and Day Two
- Key Passage: II Corinthians 11:14

Read the Key Passage and write down how it applies to your life.

Key Box
Satan is the enemy of God's people. He is the father of lies (John 8:44). He can be either obvious in his strategies or subtle in his deception. Joshua was deceived by the Gibeonites because he did not consult with the Lord. Satan can deceive us just as he did Joshua. Therefore, we must be alert to his lies that are both obvious and subtle.

The Gibeonites knew enough about God's Word to the Israelites to use it to their advantage to deceive the Israelites into making a treaty with them. They were fully aware that God had told the Israelites to kill all of the people in Canaan so that they would not fall prey to worshiping the Canaanite gods. The Gibeonites knew that the God of Israel had proved to be a powerful God bringing victory to them.

Joshua made a treaty of peace with the Gibeonites because he believed

> a lie. We all have at one time or another made a poor decision based on false information or on information based on "half-truths." As Christians, we can be deceived by false information which twists God's Word or uses it against us.

What stood out to you as you read the Key Box?

Read the scriptures below. When answering the questions, reflect on the theme of this section: *Satan, the Father of Lies*. When you write your answers, ask yourself how this applies to your life or your life experiences.

Joshua 9

What tactics did the Gibeonites use to deceive Joshua?

What did the men of Israel fail to do (v. 14)?

How would you have responded to the lies that the Gibeonites told Joshua?

I Peter 5:6-9
What do you think Peter means when he refers to Satan as *a roaring lion?*

II Corinthians 11:13-14
What do you think Paul means when he refers to Satan *as an angel of light?*

Which tactic do you think that Satan uses most often on committed Christians?

Matthew 4:5-7
Describe the tactic the enemy used against Jesus in this passage.

How did Jesus counterattack?

Describe a time when this has happened to you.

II Timothy 2:15
What does this verse mean to you when it exhorts you to handle God's Word correctly?

II. Joshua's Mistake
- Day Three and Day Four
- Key Passage: Joshua 9:14

Read the Key Passage and write down how it applies to your life.

Key Box
Joshua evaluated the team of Gibeonites by what he saw. He chose to walk by sight and not by faith and failed to consult with the Lord. We

too are tempted to make decisions only on the evidence of what we see. Joshua was a great leader, yet he failed to seek the Lord before he made the decision to make a treaty with the Gibeonites. Like Joshua, we need to learn to continually seek God's will in each decision.

What stood out to you as you read the Key Box?

_____

_____

_____

Read the scriptures below. When answering the questions, reflect on the theme of this section: *Joshua's Mistake*. When you write your answers, ask yourself how this applies to your life or your life experiences.

Hebrews 1:11
Why is it so difficult for us to walk by faith?

_____

_____

_____

What do we need to do to avoid making decisions only on what we see and feel?

_____

_____

_____

James 1:5-6
What must we do to assure ourselves that we will not be deceived?

_____

Why do we find it easier to rely on our own wisdom?

Why do you think that Joshua did not consult with the Lord before he made a treaty with the Gibeonites?

Describe a time in your life when you acted impulsively without first going to the Lord.

Matthew 6:33
What should you use as a guide in making your decisions?

Joshua: Posessing the Land

III.   Redeemed Mistakes
- Day Five and Day Six
- Key Passage: Romans 8:28

Read the Key Passage and write down how it applies to your life.

Key Box
Joshua made a peace treaty with the Gibeonites and swore to it by an oath in the name of the God of Israel. Joshua could not revoke his word once he knew that he had been deceived because he had sealed it in the name of God. The Gibeonites were clever in that they knew that once Joshua took an oath, he would not break it. Fortunately, God is the "Redeemer" and will redeem our mistakes when we turn to Him. Because the Gibeonites had not been honest with Joshua, he determined that they would thereafter be woodcutters and water carriers, and later temple servants. The scriptures tell us that there were 500 Nephilim (Gibeonites) who returned to Jerusalem after the Babylonian captivity, suggesting that the Gibeonites did become devoted to the Lord.

What stood out to you as you read the Key Box?

_____
_____
_____
_____

Read the scriptures below. When answering the questions, reflect on the theme of this section: *Redeemed Mistakes*. When you write your answers, ask yourself how this applies to your life or your life experiences.

Joshua 9:20, 27; I Chronicles 9:1-2
How did God turn Joshua's mistake of making a treaty with the enemy into something good?

_____
_____

75

Describe a time in your life when the Lord turned a mistake you made into good.

I John 1:9
How should we respond when we make a mistake?

Life Applications
- Ask the Lord to help you correctly handle His word so that you are less vulnerable to Satan's attacks.
- Determine always to seek first God's will and to be obedient to what He wants you to do.
- Remember that God is the "Redeemer" and longs to use you – mistakes and all – for His glory!

Prayer
Lord Jesus,

Keep me from following my own ways and not obeying Your Word. I pray that You would redeem my mistakes as I turn to You in repentance. Thank you that You made a way on the cross so that I could be forgiven. Lead me in Your everlasting ways.

In Jesus' Name,
Amen

Notes

Joanne Ellison

CONQUERING THE LAND
LESSON NINE
JOSHUA 10 THROUGH 12

Meditation
Do not be afraid or discouraged because of this vast army. For the battle is not yours, but God's. II Chronicles 20:15

Main Theme
When Joshua remembers to consult with the Lord in his battles, God brings him victory. God will conquer the enemies in our spiritual life if we remember to seek His counsel and rely on His strength and intervention. Sometimes we question whether or not God is on our side. The real question to ask is, are we on God's side?

Lesson Focus
Read *Joshua 10, 11, and 12*

I. Ongoing Warfare
- Day One and Day Two
- Key Passage: Ephesians 6:12

Read the Key Passage and write down how it applies to your life.

_____
_____
_____
_____

Key Box
Joshua faced ongoing warfare as he led the Israelites in taking possession of the Promised Land. He learned the importance of obedience and of depending on God for the victory. Whenever we are on God's side, we face opposition. Today, as we face opposition in our walk with the Lord, we must learn to depend on God and to follow in His ways.

What stood out to you as you read the Key Box?

Read the scriptures below. When answering the questions, reflect on the theme of this section: *Ongoing Warfare*. When you write your answers, ask yourself how this applies to your life or your life experiences.

I Timothy 6:12
What do you think Paul means when he tells us to fight the good fight of faith?

Ephesians 6:10-12
Whom does Paul tell you that you are struggling against in your spiritual battles?

How does knowing this affect your view of the conflicts you have in different situations and with other people?

Joanne Ellison

I Samuel 17:47; Psalm 24:8
Who should you let fight your battles for you?

In your spiritual life, how can you have the assurance that God is fighting your battles?

II. The Enemy Destroyed
- Day Three and Day Four
- Key Passage: Joshua 10:24

Read the Key Passage and write down how it applies to your life.

Key Box
Ancient kings often placed their feet on their enemies to demonstrate their conquering power over them. Joshua told the commanders of the Israelite army to put their feet on the necks of the enemy kings who were captured.

Jesus disarmed the power and authority of the evil one when He died on the cross. He put the enemy under His feet signifying His conquering power over Satan, death, and sin.

Joshua: Posessing the Land

> Although the ultimate defeat of the enemy has been accomplished, until that day of Christ's return, the enemy still prowls around trying to disrupt our lives. In the gospel of Matthew, Jesus provides a description of the kingdom of heaven and the enemy's attempts to destroy His kingdom.

What stood out to you as you read the Key Box?

_____

_____

_____

_____

Read the scriptures below. When answering the questions, reflect on the theme of this section: *The Enemy Destroyed*. When you write your answers, ask yourself how this applies to your life or your life experiences.

Matthew 13:24-29
What did the enemy sow in the good field?

_____

_____

_____

_____

What are some weeds that are hindering growth in your life?

_____

_____

_____

_____

Why is it important in our spiritual lives to destroy the weeds?

_____

Deuteronomy 7:16
Why did Joshua completely destroy the enemy in each land he conquered?

I Corinthians 15:20-28
How does this passage relate to the defeat of sin and death in our lives?

Colossians 2:13-15
How did God triumph and accomplish the ultimate defeat over the enemy?

III. The Encouragement of God
- Day Five and Day Six
- Key Passage: Joshua 10:25

Read the Key Passage and write down how it applies to your life.

Key Box
The word encouragement is defined as "to put heart into." God continued to speak encouraging words to Joshua throughout his battles. He does that for us as well.

Another way that God encouraged the Israelites other than by offering words of encouragement was by demonstrating His supernatural power when He made the sun stand still. Today, we need to take time to recognize His awesome power at work in our universe.

What stood out to you as you read the Key Box?

Read the scriptures below. When answering the questions, reflect on the theme of this section: *The Encouragement of God*. When you write your answers, ask yourself how this applies to your life or your life experiences.

Joshua 10:8
How does God speak encouragement to us when we are going through the battles of life?

What are some of the ways that the enemy attempts to discourage you?

How does Satan try to keep you from recognizing God's presence in your life?

Joshua 10:12-14
Tell about a time when God intervened in your life and did something for you that seemed humanly impossible.

Joshua 11:23
What encouragement do we have when we allow God to fight our battles?

Life Applications
- Remember the battle belongs to the Lord. God is our refuge and our strength and He encourages us as we follow His leading.
- As you identify situations that seem to cause spiritual battles in your life, take them to God in prayer.
- Note the steps that you feel God is leading you to take in conquering your personal battles.

Prayer

Dear Lord,

Help me to rely on Your strength to fight the battles that I face, remembering that the battle belongs to You. I commit to follow You and to seek You in all that I do trusting that You will protect me.

In Jesus' Name,
Amen

Notes

Joshua: Posessing the Land

DIVIDING THE LAND
LESSON TEN
JOSHUA 13 THROUGH 19

Meditation
...How long will you wait before you begin to take possession of the land that the Lord, the God of your fathers, has given you? Joshua 18:3

Main Theme
The Lord gave the Promised Land to the Israelites. He went before them to defeat the enemies in the land. The Israelites had to go in, however, to claim the land. God has given us His promises, and it is our responsibility to claim them and walk in victory. In order to walk in faith and claim the promises of God, we must remember to go in God's strength. The Lord called Moses to lead the people out of Egypt and he gave him the strength to do it. The Lord then called Joshua to lead the people into the Promised Land and he remained strong even at the age of 85 (Joshua 14:11)! So often we allow the enemy to take land that is our inheritance or we refuse to lay hold of the promises of God because they seem unattainable. The Lord instructed Joshua to go and take the land that was the inheritance of the Israelites. It belonged to them according to God but they needed to lay hold of it. Each tribe was given a portion of the land and no one was forgotten or left behind. Beloved children of God, we too have an inheritance in Christ. We must lay hold of the promises in His Word and remember that He will strengthen us as we walk in faith to claim our inheritance.

Lesson Focus
Read Joshua *13 through 19*.

I. Accomplishing God's Purpose through His Strength
- Day One and Day Two
- Key Passage: Joshua 14:10

Read the Key Passage and write down how it applies to your life.

Joanne Ellison

Key Box
When we depend on God, He gives us strength for each season of our lives. He is not concerned with how old we are in numeric terms. He is concerned with how mature we are in Him. Throughout our lives, the Lord calls us to serve Him as part of His army of soldiers. We never retire from God's army. Joshua was over 85 years old when the Lord spoke to him in Joshua 13:1. Large areas of land still needed to be taken. In addition, these lands needed to be divided up among the tribes.

Joshua and the apostle Paul both knew that their years were numbered, yet, a vast amount of work remained to be accomplished to fulfill God's purposes. Throughout their lives, both continue to fight the battles that were before them. Joshua continued to work into his old age to fulfill what God had called him to do. I imagine there were times when both men were tired or discouraged or felt like giving up before their tasks were completed. Yet, God gave them the strength to persevere.

The Lord has numbered our days and has given us all a purpose to glorify Him on this earth and to spread His Word. As I write these questions, I feel as though there are not enough hours in the day. Yet, the Lord reassures me that *I can seek Him and His strength*, that *I can do all things in Christ who strengthens me*, and that *He will renew my strength each day*. As I depend on Him, I will be able to accomplish those things He would have me to do.

What stood out to you as you read the Key Box?

Read the scriptures below. When answering the questions, reflect on the theme of this section: *Accomplishing God's Purpose through His*

Strength. When you write your answers, ask yourself how this applies to your life or your life experiences.

Luke 14:25-35
What is the cost of being a disciple of Christ?

_____

_____

_____

II Corinthians 11:16-33
In what ways did Paul describe the cost he paid as a disciple of Christ?

_____

_____

_____

What is the personal cost to you in being a disciple of Christ?

_____

_____

_____

Isaiah 40:27-31
What does God give us so that we, like Paul, are able to continue to *fight the good fight?*

_____

_____

_____

Philippians 4:13
In what way does Paul say that God helped him to accomplish his task of spreading the gospel?

What has God asked you to do that requires spiritual strength?

What holds you back from believing that God will supply you with all that you need to fulfill His purposes?

II. Our Inheritance
- Day Three and Day Four
- Key Passage: Psalm 16:5-6

Read the Key Passage and write down how it applies to your life.

Joshua: Posessing the Land

Key Box

In Scripture, we often see actual events, both natural and historical, that point to spiritual truths.

In the Old Testament, we see God fulfilling His promise to Abraham to form the nation of Israel. Then, He guided them to the Promised Land which was their inheritance. As a part of the inheritance which God promised Abraham, a new society was being established that contrasted greatly with the existing Canaanite society. New boundaries were established as the land was being parceled out to the tribes. The tribes had the responsibility to share the land for the benefit of all the people.

In our spiritual lives, the Lord is our inheritance. The Lord continues to draw us to Himself with cords of love. The Holy Spirit is establishing in us the Lord's boundaries in our spiritual land. Jesus longs to be recognized as sovereign Lord and King of Kings. Through faith in Him and His resurrection, we are made heirs of God.

What stood out to you as you read the Key Box?

_____

_____

_____

Read the scriptures below. When answering the questions, reflect on the theme of this section: *Our Inheritance*. When you write your answers, ask yourself how this applies to your life or your life experiences.

Deuteronomy 18:1-2; Joshua 13:8 – 14:5

When the Lord divided Canaan among the tribes of Israel, why do you think the Levites did not receive land?

_____

_____

_____

91

How does this action apply to us today?

What was the merit of dividing the land with specific boundaries?

Psalm 16
How does King David describe his boundaries?

Describe a time in your life when you drew your own boundary lines of control, instead of allowing the Lord to set up His Kingdom in your life.

Describe a time when you allowed the Lord to establish His boundaries in your life, and tell what happened.

Ephesians 1:13-14
What is the deposit on our inheritance?

III. Turning Complaints into Constructive Action
- Day Five and Day Six
- Key Passage: Joshua 17:14

Read the Key Passage and write down how it applies to your life.

Key Box
Miriam and Aaron complained about Moses' wife being a Cushite. Their complaining turned into judgment of Moses and his ability to lead. Many times as they traveled through the desert, the children of Israel complained. Even after they were in the Promised Land, the tribe of Joseph complained because they wanted more land. They feared they didn't have enough land for the numbers in their tribe and they feared the Canaanites who had chariots and power.

Too often, we, like the Israelites of old, are guilty of complaining about what we do, what we don't have, and many other things. The Lord also tells us to stop complaining and to use the resources He gives us in the best way we can.

What stood out to you as you read the Key Box?

Read the scriptures below. When answering the questions, reflect on the theme of this section: *Turning Complaints into Constructive Action*. When you write your answers, ask yourself how this applies to your life or your life experiences.

Joshua 17:14-18
Why did the children of Joseph complain?

What did Joshua tell the children of Joseph when they complained because they wanted more land?

In what areas of your life do you do the most complaining?

Colossians 3:15-17
What is the anecdote to discontentment?

I Peter 4:7-10
Based on this passage, what are the attitudes we should have in our lives?

Numbers 12:1-15
Since complaining is like leprosy or a cancer that spreads, what can you do to curtail the tendency to complain?

Philippians 4:10-13
Why does Paul encourage the Philippians to *do everything without complaining?*

Life Applications
- Acknowledge daily that the Lord is all you need.
- Recognize that His boundaries are safe and secure.
- Identify areas in your life where the Lord is asking you to have a grateful heart instead of a complaining heart.
- Ask the Lord to help you make the best use of the resources He has given you.
- Claim His precious promises for you.

Prayer

You are my portion, O Lord; I have promised to obey your words. I have sought your face with all my heart; be gracious to me according to your promise.

Psalm 119:57

Notes

Joanne Ellison

CITIES OF REFUGE
LESSON ELEVEN
JOSHUA 20

Meditation
God is our refuge and strength, an ever-present help in trouble. Psalm 46:1

Main Theme
The cities of refuge foreshadow the place of refuge Christ promises us. From Genesis through Revelation, God has provided a refuge for those who obey His ways. Today, just as in the days of old, the Lord is waiting for us to run to Him with our troubles. He is our place of refuge. Jesus died to deliver us from our sins. As our Lord and Savior, He continues to be for us our place of safety as we walk with Him.

Lesson Focus
Read *Joshua 20*.

I. God's Law: Thou Shall Not Kill
- Day One and Day Two
- Key Passage: Matthew 5:21-26

Read the Key Passage and write down how it applies to your life.

_____

_____

_____

_____

Key Box
Exodus 20:13 states, *You shall not murder.* God laid down the law in Genesis 9:5-6 that those who shed blood should pay for their crime with their own blood. The Bible, however, distinguishes between murder (premeditated and deliberate) and involuntary manslaughter (accidental, without hostility) (Deuteronomy 19:5). God demonstrated His love for us by sending His Son to die for our sins. If we have accepted Jesus' sacrificial death and offer of forgiveness, we have been justified by His blood and saved from God's wrath. As

Joshua: Posessing the Land

believers, when we sin but truly turn back to the Lord, His blood again covers us and cleanses us from our sin (I John 1:9). There are still consequences for sin, both spiritually and legally. The laws of our land establish the consequences for our illegal actions. The scriptures explain the spiritual consequences for our sin.

What stood out to you as you read the Key Box?

_____

_____

_____

Read the scriptures below. When answering the questions, reflect on the theme of this section: *God's Law: Thou Shall Not Kill*. When you write your answers, ask yourself how this applies to your life or your life experiences.

Genesis 4:1-12
What did the Lord tell Cain were the consequences for killing his brother, Abel?

_____

_____

_____

Why do you think that the Lord offered protection for Cain?

_____

_____

_____

Genesis 9:4-6
What is the reason that God commands man not to commit murder?

99

How do you see the disregard for life in our society today?

What statement does that make in regard to how life is valued?

Matthew 5:21-26
How does Jesus equate anger with murder?

In recent memory, whom have you murdered with your anger?

What must you do to make restitution?

_____
_____
_____
_____

II. Cities of Refuge
- Day Three and Day Four
- Key Passage: Joshua 21:1-2

Read the Key Passage and write down how it applies to your life.

_____
_____
_____
_____

Key Box
In the Old Testament, many legal and judicial decisions were transacted just "inside" the city gates. Jesus was crucified "outside" the city gates. His death completed the transaction of exchanging the law of sin and death for the law of grace. The penalty for our sins is death, but Jesus gave His blood (His life) for us when He was crucified outside of the city gates. He became our place of refuge, protection, and life.

What stood out to you as you read the Key Box?

_____
_____
_____

Read the scriptures below. When answering the questions, reflect on the theme of this section: *Cities of Refuge*. When you write your answers, ask yourself how this applies to your life or your life experiences.

Joshua 20:1-4
Why did the Lord tell Joshua to designate cities of refuge?

What appears to be the purpose or significance of the entrance to the city gate?

How is God our refuge and our strength?

Numbers 35:6-15; Deuteronomy 19:1-7
Where do you run in times of trouble?

What is your first source of help?

Matthew 5:17; Hebrews 13:10-13
What do you think is the spiritual significance that Jesus, representing our place of refuge, was crucified outside of the city gates?

III. Finding Refuge in Jesus
- Day Five and Day Six
- Key Passage: Matthew 11:28-31

Read the Key Passage and write down how it applies to your life.

Key Box
Jesus carries our burdens. He tells us in Matthew that His yoke is easy and His burden is light. A yoke is a wooden harness that fits over the shoulders of a pair of oxen. Jesus tells us to be yoked with Him. I realized recently that I was carrying some heavy burdens. This passage reminded me that Jesus was willing to carry my burdens, but I needed to let go and allow Him to carry them. Jesus is always waiting on us to come to Him.

We are sometimes like fugitives running from our own fears, lack of trust, or other obstacles in our lives. Just as the roads were marked and in good repair to the cities of refuge, so the Lord has made a way for us that is free and clear. He longs for us to run to Him.

What stood out to you as you read the Key Box?

Read the scriptures below. When answering the questions, reflect on the theme of this section: *Finding Refuge in Jesus*. When you write your answers, ask yourself how this applies to your life or your life experiences.

Hebrews 6:13-20
How does this passage apply to you in describing Jesus as a place of safety, refuge, and love?

How does knowing this help you in your daily life?

What causes you to feel burdened by circumstances in your life?

What practical things can you do to allow the Lord to be your strength?

Matthew 11:28-30
What does Jesus promise that we will find if we *take His yoke upon us?*

John 6:37
If you have struggled with such things as fear, rejection, or loneliness what must you do to receive Jesus' love and allow Him to be a place of refuge for you?

Life Applications
- Ask the Lord to show you what burdens you are carrying.
- Ask Him to enable you to see that there are no roadblocks separating Him from you.
- Review the **Meditation** for the week.

Prayer
And I pray that Christ will be more and more at home in your hearts living within you as you trust in Him. May your roots go down deep into the soil of God's marvelous love, and may you be able to feel and understand, as all God's children should, how long, how wide, how deep, and how high His love really is, and to experience this love for yourselves, though it is so great that you will never see the end of it or fully know or understand it.

Ephesians 3:17-18 Living Bible

Notes

Joanne Ellison

SPIRITUAL COMMUNITIES
LESSON TWELVE
JOSHUA 21

Meditation
Let us not give up meeting together, as some are in the habit of doing, but let us encourage one another... Hebrews 10:25

Main Theme
God divinely appointed cities throughout the Promised Land that He gave to the Levites. These cities provided spiritual communities for the Israelites. As believers, the church provides us with a spiritual community: a place to worship, to learn, to grow spiritually, and to enter into God's rest. It is through Christian communities that we are strengthened and encouraged in our faith and therefore it is important that we are part of a community of believers. During difficult times my Christian friends have been a source of comfort to me. God provided spiritual communities for the Israelites because He knew that they would need one another to grow spiritually. We too need the love, hope, and strength that our fellow brothers and sisters in Christ offer us.

Lesson Focus
Read *Joshua 21*.

I. Priesthood of Believers
- Day One and Day Two
- Key Passage: I Peter 2:4-10

Read the Key Passage and write down how it applies to your life.

_____

_____

_____

Key Box
The tribe of Levi consisted of three main branches corresponding to Levi's three sons: Kohath, Gershon, and Merari. Moses and Aaron

were of the Kohathite branch. Each branch had duties to perform in the physical and spiritual care of the tabernacle.

Throughout the study of Joshua, we see natural and spiritual events taking place. We have compared these things to our spiritual lives. As we examine the Levitical priests of the Old Testament, we gain insight as believers into how we should worship, develop spiritually, and how we are to care for the temple of the Lord.

What stood out to you as you read the Key Box?

_____

_____

_____

_____

Read the scriptures below. When answering the questions, reflect on the theme of this section: *Priesthood of Believers*. When you write your answers, ask yourself how this applies to your life or your life experiences.

Numbers 3:14-37
Describe the duties that the Kohathite, the Gershonite, and the Merarite clans performed in the care of the tabernacle.

_____

_____

_____

_____

Compare the duties of the Kohathites, the Gershonites, and the Merarites to our spiritual duties.

_____

_____

_____

_____

I Peter 2:4-10
How does this passage describe believers?

_____

_____

_____

_____

II Corinthians 6:16
What does it mean to be the *temple of the living God?*

_____

_____

_____

_____

II. Spiritual Communities
- Day Three and Day Four
- Key Passage: Matthew 5:13-14

Read the Key Passage and write down how it applies to your life.

_____

_____

_____

_____

Key Box
When the Tent of Meeting was set up at Shiloh, the duties of the Levites underwent change. Although the tabernacle remained at Shiloh until the time of Samuel (I Samuel 4:3), it is significant to note that the spiritual leaders were dispersed throughout the entire land and not just concentrated in one place.

The Lord continues to give us "spiritual communities" throughout the world where we can learn from one another and grow spiritually.

Joshua: Posessing the Land

> We are the "priesthood of believers," and the Lord wants us to be "salt and light" to a hurting world.

What stood out to you as you read the Key Box?

Read the scriptures below. When answering the questions, reflect on the theme of this section: *Spiritual Communities*. When you write your answers, ask yourself how this applies to your life or your life experiences.

Joshua 18:1, Joshua 21:1-3

Why do you think it was important for the Levites to be dispersed throughout the Promised Land?

Why do you think that it is important for us as part of Christ's Body, the Church, to be dispersed throughout our communities?

Why do you think that we have a tendency to want to stay with our spiritual friends, instead of trying to be *salt and light* to the world?

Hebrews 10:25
Why is it important to meet together as a body?

I Timothy 4:9-14; II Timothy 4:1-5
Describe in your own words how I and II Timothy instruct us to be effective witnesses within the spiritual community.

What does the passage in I Timothy teach us to do?

III. Spiritual Rest
- Day Five and Day Six
- Key Passage: Psalm 91:1-2

Read the Key Passage and write down how it applies to your life.

Joshua: Posessing the Land

> **Key Box**
> As we grow in our walk with Christ, we experience times when we must battle against those things that oppose our walk, but as with Joshua, the Lord will fulfill His promises. He assures us that *He will be with us wherever we go (Joshua 1:9)*.

What stood out to you as you read the Key Box?

_____
_____
_____

Read the scriptures below. When answering the questions, reflect on the theme of this section: *Spiritual Rest*. When you write your answers, ask yourself how this applies to your life or your life experiences.

Joshua 21:43-45
How does the Lord give Israel rest?

_____
_____
_____

What can you do in your spiritual walk to maintain a place of rest?

_____
_____
_____

Exodus 33:12-14
What was Moses' key to finding rest?

I Kings 5:1-7
What enabled King Solomon to find rest on all sides?

What gives us confidence to rest in the Lord?

Psalm 62:1-8
Even though David experienced wars during his reign, what was his attitude towards the Lord?

Isaiah 26:3-4
Whether we are experiencing spiritual battles or whether we are in a peaceful season in our walk with Christ, what should our attitude be?

Jeremiah 6:16
How do we find rest for our souls?

What do you think Jeremiah means by *the ancient path?*

Life Applications
- Describe what you can do to enter into God's rest.
- Be intentional about entering God's rest.
- Read and reflect on Hebrews 4:8-11.

Prayer
Heavenly Father,

Thank you for providing me with a spiritual community. Help me to be salt and light to the world and protect me from activity that prevents me from relationships.

In Jesus' Name,
Amen.

Joanne Ellison

Notes

Joshua: Posessing the Land

TRANSITIONS
LESSON THIRTEEN
JOSHUA 22

Meditation
Stand at the crossroads and look; ask for the ancient paths, ask where the good way is, and walk in it, and you will find rest for your souls. Jeremiah 6:16

Main Theme
As you read the Main Theme, underline words or thoughts most meaningful to you.

In our lives, we will always experience change. Transitions in our life can produce anxiety. If we keep our focus on the Lord and look for His path, we will be at rest during those times of change. Jeremiah 6:16 states that we must *stand at the crossroads and look, asking for the ancient paths and where the good way is.* When we find God's path we will find ourselves at peace. It is often difficult to know which way the Lord is directing you, but His Word is clear that if we seek Him we will find Him. *I know the plans I have for you, declares the Lord, plans to prosper you and not to harm you, plans to give you hope and a future. Then you will call upon me and come and pray to me and I will listen to you. You will seek me and find me when you seek me with all your heart* (Jeremiah 29:11-13). Joshua led the Israelites into the Promised Land and now they had entered into a new season of establishing themselves in another land --- the land of promise. They needed direction as they began their new lives together. As believers there are transitional times in our lives and we must remember that the Lord has plans for our good that are full of hope and our future.

Lesson Focus
Read *Joshua 22*.

I. Transitions
- Day One and Day Two
- Key Passage: Joshua 22:4

Read the Key Passage and write down how it applies to your life.

> **Key Box**
> The tribes of Reuben, Gad, and the half-tribe of Manassah returned to the eastern side of the Jordan. They had fulfilled their promise to Moses and Joshua in assuring that the other tribes had a secure foothold in the land west of the Jordan. Therefore, the time had come for them to leave the other nine and one-half tribes and go back to their families. The common task of securing the land had kept all of the tribes unified.
>
> The relationships that the tribes of Israel had experienced would never again be the same. Change can be bittersweet, evoking both happy and sad emotions. Death, illness, divorce, and job changes produce many different emotions. The Lord directs us in His Word on how we can remain stable as we go through these changes.

What stood out to you as you read the Key Box?

Read the scriptures below. When answering the questions, reflect on the theme of this section: *Transitions*. When you write your answers, ask yourself how this applies to your life or your life experiences.
Deuteronomy 31:6; Joshua 1:9; Psalm 94:14; Isaiah 49:14-16

How do the scriptures assure you that God really loves you?

Joshua 22:5
What does Joshua tell the Israelites is of the utmost importance during times of transition?

In times of transition, what influences the way we adapt to change?

What are some of the reasons that transition produces anxiety in us?

How can our faith make a difference in times of transition?

II. Rumors
- Day Three and Day Four
- Key Passage: Joshua 22:10-13

Read the Key Passage and write down how it applies to your life.

Key Box
A true accounting of events can help clarify a situation, but a false accounting can turn into a rumor and create a volatile situation. The tribes that crossed back to the east side of the Jordan built an altar as a memorial or "witness" to remind future generations that they worshiped the one true God. They feared the possible apostasy of future generations who might forget the commandments of the Lord. The other Israelite tribes, however, thought that they were setting up a separate altar, which had been forbidden.

The nine-and-one-half tribes sent Phinehas and a representative from each of the tribes to find out if the other tribes were "breaking faith." The representatives told the tribes of their concerns and listened to and accepted their reply. Bringing controversies into the light weakens the position of the enemy, not allowing him to gain a foothold into the situation.

What stood out to you as you read the Key Box?

Read the scriptures below. When answering the questions, reflect on the theme of this section: *Rumors*. When you write your answers, ask yourself how this applies to your life or your life experiences.

Deuteronomy 13:12-15
What were the Israelites told to do if corrupt men were influencing the people to worship other gods?

Why do you think that the nine and one-half tribes were ready to go to war against the two and one-half tribes who settled east of Jordan after hearing that they had built an altar?

Numbers 25
Describe the sins and their consequences when Israel worshiped another god.

Ephesians 4:25-31
Explain how being truthful and trying to get to the "bottom of things" proves to be extremely beneficial.

I Corinthians 6:1-3
How do you think you should handle controversy in your life, particularly when you feel that you have been wronged or falsely accused?

I Thessalonians 5:21
What does it mean to *test everything?*

III. Peacemakers
- Day Five and Day Six
- Key Passage: Matthew 5:9

Read the Key Passage and write down how it applies to your life.

Key Box
The lesson today is really a story about peacemakers. Commentator John Huffman writes, "Peace, combined with truth, is the highest priority; without truth, it is a compromise. Truth without a desire for peace is brittle legalism." You may have heard it said that it is better to have peace at all costs, but when we aim to have peace without truth, we pay a high price because in the end, there is no real peace.

Jesus said, *Blessed are the peacemakers.* He challenges each one of us to stop, look for the truth, and listen. These are traits that help us to be the peacemakers that God wants us to be.

What stood out to you as you read the Key Box?

Read the scriptures below. When answering the questions, reflect on the theme of this section: *Peacemakers*. When you write your answers, ask yourself how this applies to your life or your life experiences.

Numbers 25:10-13
After reading the story in Numbers 25, how do you think that Phinehas' actions enabled him to become a peacemaker for God?

Using this story as a guide, what do you think it takes for us to be true Biblical peacemakers?

James 3:17-18; Zechariah 8:14-19
What do you think these scriptures teach us about being a peacemaker?

What must you do to help you to be the kind of peacemaker that these scriptures describe?

_____

_____

_____

_____

Life Applications
- In a time of transition, remember that God promises He will always be with you and never forsake you.
- Seek out ways that you can apply the scriptures in this lesson to your life.
- Pray that the Lord will give you wisdom as you try to discern between truth and rumor.
- Determine to be a peacemaker in God's way, which embraces both truth and peace.

Prayer
Heavenly Father,

As I move into times of transition, I pray that You will give me the grace to trust You for You alone are trustworthy and faithful to all of Your promises. I pray that You will give me wisdom to discern between truth and rumor, and to give me the courage and determination to be a peacemaker embracing truth and peace.

In Jesus' Name,
Amen.

Notes

Joanne Ellison

FAITHFULNESS AND OBEDIENCE
LESSON FOURTEEN
JOSHUA 23

Meditation
If you fully obey the Lord your God and carefully follow all of His commands I give you today, the Lord your God will set you high above all the nations on earth. Deuteronomy 28:1

Main Theme
Joshua reminds the Israelites of God's faithfulness. We also see Joshua's faithful response to God throughout His life, and his exhortation to the Israelites to respond to God with obedience. As God touches our lives with His faithfulness, we must respond with obedience in order to reap the blessings and promises of God.

Lesson Focus
Read *Joshua 23*.

I. God's Covenant of Faithfulness
- Day One and Day Two
- Key Passage: Genesis 17:4-7

Read the Key Passage and write down how it applies to your life.

___

___

___

___

Key Box
The Lord promised to Abraham in Genesis 17 that he would be the father of many nations. We see the fulfillment of that promise beginning in Genesis 21 with the birth of Isaac. It required faith on the part of Abraham and Sarah to believe that the Lord would fulfill His promise to them. In fact, Abraham and Sarah initially laughed when they heard that two people their age would have a child. Sarah even tried to fulfill the promise herself by giving her servant Hagar to

> Abraham to produce the promised child.
>
> As believers, we enter into a covenant with God to obey His Word and to enter into His promises. Often, we struggle with believing these promises. We try to control situations, rather than choosing to trust the Lord and allow Him to fulfill His promises.

What stood out to you as you read the Key Box?

_____
_____
_____
_____

Read the scriptures below. When answering the questions, reflect on the theme of this section: *God's Covenant of Faithfulness*. When you write your answers, ask yourself how this applies to your life or your life experiences.

Genesis 3:26-29
What does Paul mean when he says, *If you belong to Christ, then you are Abraham's seed?*

_____
_____
_____
_____

In our spiritual lives, what is the benefit of being "Abraham's seed?"

_____
_____
_____
_____

What must you do to let go and wait patiently on God, allowing Him to work things out for you?

Joanne Ellison

_____

_____

_____

Joshua 23:3-14
How was God faithful to His covenant people?

_____

_____

_____

II. Our Obedience and Faithfulness
- Day Three and Day Four
- Key Passage: Joshua 23:6

Read the Key Passage and write down how it applies to your life.

_____

_____

_____

Key Box
When someone is about to die, we usually pay extra attention to what he or she has to say. I remember a few days before my grandfather died, he told me that he thought he was going to die. Of course, I told him that he should not talk that way, but when he repeated it to me, I began to pay attention. Shortly before Jesus died, He prayed to God the Father (John 17). We pay special attention to these words. When Joshua knew that he was going to die soon, he gave the Israelites their final instructions. We, too, should take note of these final admonitions. As children of God, we are grafted into the same covenant with Him, and therefore, have the same call to obedience if we are to receive the privileges and blessings of God.

Joshua: Posessing the Land

> Joshua emphasizes that the Israelites must refuse to ally themselves with the enemy who remains in the land. We sometimes find ourselves making peace with our enemies when the Lord wants us to destroy them. Our enemies can be gossip, jealousy, poor stewardship, lying, etc. The world today is full of these things, but we are not to ally ourselves with them.

What stood out to you as you read the Key Box?

___

Read the scriptures below. When answering the questions, reflect on the theme of this section: *Our Obedience and Faithfulness.* When you write your answers, ask yourself how this applies to your life or your life experiences.

Joshua 23

According to *Joshua*, what are the three things that the Israelites must do in order for the Lord to continue to fight their battles?

___

How can you apply this scripture to the battles you face today?

___

Describe in your own words what Joshua 23:12-13 says if we ally ourselves with the enemies of God.

129

What things compromise your loyalty to the Lord?

Describe a time when you have been ensnared by these things (v. 13)?

I Timothy 4:9-14
What is the prescription that aids living a life of faith and obedience?

II Timothy 3:16-17
How does scripture help us to live obedient lives?

Where have you been in disobedience to God's Word and need to adhere to correction?

III. From Obedience to Love
- Day Five and Day Six
- Key Passage: Joshua 23:10-11

Read the Key Passage and write down how it applies to your life.

Key Box
Christ set us free from the law of sin when He died on the cross. This was and is His greatest gift of love to us. He gave His all for us, so how can we do less than give our all to Him?

As we give Him our love, we need to remember that love and obedience go hand in hand. Just as children are more willing to obey when they know that they are loved we return God's love through obedience.

What stood out to you as you read the Key Box?

Read the scriptures below. When answering the questions, reflect on the theme of this section: *From Obedience to Love*. When you write your answers, ask yourself how this applies to your life or your life experiences.

Deuteronomy 6:5; Deuteronomy 10:12-13; Deuteronomy 11:1; Matthew 22:37-38

According to the scriptures above, what is the greatest commandment?

What is the natural outflow of loving God?

John 14:15-24
Who did Jesus send to help us to be obedient, and how does knowing that help us in our daily lives (v. 16)?

What does Jesus tell us the Father will do if we are obedient? (v.23)

What do you think it means for Jesus to "make His home in us?"

Life Applications
- Share any feelings with the Lord that are hindering your spiritual growth.
- Ask Him to forgive, cleanse, and heal you.
- Journal these feelings.
- Wait patiently and then refer to your journal to see how God is working in your life.

Prayer
Heavenly Father,

Thank You for Your covenant of faithfulness. You have been faithful throughout the generations. I pray that I may be faithful to obey Your Word, and be willing to submit to correction when I have been disobedient. Help me to obey You out of love and surrender out of trust.

In Jesus' Name,
Amen

Notes

Joshua: Posessing the Land

WHOM WILL YOU SERVE?
LESSON FIFTEEN
JOSHUA 24

Meditation
...But as for me and my household, we will serve the Lord. Joshua 24:15

Main Theme
Joshua chose to serve the Lord. He addressed the Israelites for the last time and urged them to make the same choice, that of serving the true God. Today, we are faced with that same choice: to fear God and serve Him or serve other gods. Other gods can be anything in our lives that we make more important than our love for God.

Lesson Focus
Read *Joshua 24*.

I. Testimony About God's Faithfulness
- Day One and Day Two
- Key Passage: Joshua 24:15

Read the Key Passage and write down how it applies to your life.

_____

_____

_____

_____

Key Box
Joshua testified of the faithfulness of God to the Israelites. He recounted the goodness of the Lord as He faithfully brought them out of Egypt and led them into the Promised Land. God was also faithful to defeat all of their enemies. Joshua had followed the Lord all the days of his life and his testimony was sincere. In other words, his "walk" matched his "talk."

Jesus relates that John the Baptist testified about Him, and that He,

> too, testifies about Himself (John 5:31-36). Testimonies can be powerful tools to encourage others to place their trust in God.

What stood out to you as you read the Key Box?

Read the scriptures below. When answering the questions, reflect on the theme of this section: *Testimonies About God's Faithfulness*. When you write your answers, ask yourself how this applies to your life or your life experiences.

Exodus 20:1-17
Why do you think that in Exodus the Ten Commandments were referred to as the *Testimony*?

Exodus 25:10-22
What was the Ark of the Covenant, and why do you think that it was referred to as the *Ark of the Testimony*?

Exodus 32:16
How do the Ten Commandments testify of the living God?

John 1:32-34; Acts 26:1-32
As believers, how do we testify about Jesus?

Revelation 12:11
What is the value in our testifying about the work of Jesus Christ in our lives?

II. The Fear of the Lord
- Day Three and Day Four
- Key Passage: Joshua 24:14

Read the Key Passage and write down how it applies to your life.

Key Box
Joshua challenged the Israelites to fear the Lord because he knew that the fear of the Lord was the key to a long, prosperous life. Joshua also knew that the fear of the Lord would protect them from

following after other gods.

Sometimes, we have a limited perspective of God. We may get it from the Old Testament readings that cause us to fear Him because we think that He is revengeful, or we may have had a traumatic experience that gave rise to a limited view of God. These views hinder our spiritual journey. We must ask God to help us develop that reverential fear that creates a desire for us to know and obey Him.

What stood out to you as you read the Key Box?

Read the scriptures below. When answering the questions, reflect on the theme of this section: *The Fear of the Lord*. When you write your answers, ask yourself how this applies to your life or your life experiences.

Deuteronomy 10:12-13
What does fear of the Lord mean?

Psalm 33; Psalm 111:10; Psalm 128:1-4
What are some of the things mentioned in these Psalms that encourage us to revere the Lord?

Isaiah 33:6
What is the key to the Lord being our true foundation?

How would you describe the difference between the fear of the Lord and being afraid of the Lord?

I Samuel 12:20-25
How does knowing the character of God enable you to fear Him in the sense of revering Him, instead of being afraid of Him?

III. Power to Serve God
- Day Five and Day Six
- Key Passage: Joshua 24:19

Read the Key Passage and write down how it applies to your life.

> **Key Box**
>
> Joshua warns the children of Israel of the danger of being overconfident. He tells them that they must be careful to serve the Lord. Yet, he tells them that they will not be able to follow God in and of themselves. The Old Testament scriptures describe God as all-powerful. Just as the Israelites needed God's power to enable them to follow Him, we must depend on God's power, not our own strength, to follow His ways.
>
> Joshua knew that the Israelites needed God's power to be faithful. He did not want them to forget all the incredible things the Lord had done for them when they began to settle into the Promised Land. It is easy for us, too, to forget the Lord when things are going well for us. God often uses our times of weakness to help us to depend on *His* power. He sent His son Jesus Christ to earth to do what we were powerless to do. We were not able to bridge the gap between God and our sins. Jesus did that for us and then He left His Holy Spirit on earth to continue to empower us to follow His ways. Joshua understood what was in men's hearts and the difficulty the Israelites would have in following God's ways.

What stood out to you as you read the Key Box?

Read the scriptures below. When answering the questions, reflect on the theme of this section: *Power to Serve God*. When you write your answers, ask yourself how this applies to your life or your life experiences.

Romans 8:1-11
From what did Jesus set us free when He died on the cross?

Joshua: Posessing the Land

What was the Old Testament powerless to do?

How did Jesus set us free?

Joshua 24:19-20
What did Joshua tell them would happen to them if they rebelled against the Lord?

II Corinthians 4:7-10
What is the treasure that Paul is talking about in this passage?

Acts 1:1-8
What power was Jesus referring to that the disciples would receive to be witnesses for Christ?

How do you think this power helps you to be faithful to the Lord?

II Corinthians 12:7-10
What did Paul say about our weaknesses when we are submitted to God?

Life Applications
- Choose today whom you will serve!
- Determine to serve the Lord wholeheartedly.
- Write down your personal testimony of how you came to accept Christ as your Lord and Savior and your journey of faith thereafter.
- Be prepared to share your story in your small group.
- Consider Joshua's words to the Israelites:
    Now fear the Lord and serve Him with all faithfulness…
    But if serving the Lord seems undesirable to you, then choose for yourselves this day whom you will serve.
    Joshua 24:14-15

Prayer

Dear Lord,
Today I choose to serve You in all that I do. Help me to testify of Your goodness and strengthen me through Your Holy Spirit.

In Jesus' Name,
Amen

Notes

Joanne Ellison

REVIEWING OUR SPIRITUAL JOURNEY
LESSON SIXTEEN
REVIEW JOSHUA

I will remember the deeds off the Lord; yes, I will remember your miracles of long ago. I will meditate on all your works and consider all your mighty deeds. Psalm 77:11-12

Main Theme
We talk about getting back to the basics in the education of today's children. However, it is just as important or even more so that we get back to the basics in our spiritual journey. The three R's of a successful spiritual journey include: repentance, remembrance, and renewal. As we review our own spiritual journey, let us make sure that we are addressing each of these basics.

Lesson Focus
Review *Joshua*.

I. Reviewing Our Spiritual Journey
- Day One and Day Two
- Key Passage: Psalm 78:4

Read the Key Passage and write down how it applies to your life.

_____

_____

_____

_____

Key Box
Our study of Joshua has provided many opportunities to grow spiritually for each of us as we continue our spiritual journey. During this study, we have talked about various promises and provisions that we have because of our relationship to Jesus Christ through the Holy Spirit.

The questions in this section are designed to assist you in reviewing the insights that you have gained that will encourage and help you in

> your spiritual journey. I hope that you will go over each question and the scripture that relates to it. Consider how the lessons you have learned apply to your life.

What stood out to you as you read the Key Box?

Read the scriptures below. When answering the questions, reflect on the theme of this section: *Reviewing Our Spiritual Journey*. When you write your answers, ask yourself how this applies to your life or your life experiences.

Joshua 1:3-9
Describe what you think Joshua meant when he said that God said, *I will give you every place where you set your foot, as I promised Moses.*

How does God's encouragement to be strong and courageous in Him apply to you today?

Joshua 2:8-11
Describe how Rahab's faith that led to God's protection relates to you today.

Joshua 3:10-13
How does the way God encouraged Joshua about driving out his enemies apply to us today?

Joshua 4:19-24
How can memorial stones be used as significant reminders of God's faithfulness?

Joshua 5:9
Compare the removal of the reproach of Egypt with the removal of our places of bondage.

Joshua 6:20
How does the defeat of the city of Jericho teach us how to defeat the strongholds in our lives?

Joshua 7:10-12
How does God's command to Joshua apply in the life of believers today?

Joshua 9:14-15
What does this passage teach us is necessary to avoid deception?

Joshua 10:8
How does God's promise to Joshua encourage you in your spiritual growth?

Joshua 18:3
What does Joshua's question to the Israelites teach us about claiming God's promises?

Joshua 20:2-3
Compare the cities of refuge where the children of Israel could go for protection with our place of refuge.

Joshua 21:3
What is the relationship between the establishment of the cities for the Levites and our involvement in spiritual communities?

Joshua 22:4-5
How can knowing God help you in transitions as it did the Israelites?

Joshua 23:6
Compare Joshua's instructions to the children of Israel to the importance of God's Word as we continue in our spiritual journey.

Joshua: Posessing the Land

Joshua 24:15
How have you answered Joshua's challenge of choosing this day whom you would serve?

II. Remembering Our Spiritual Milestones
- Day Three and Day Four
- Key Passage: I Chronicles 16:12

Read the Key Passage and write down how it applies to your life.

Key Box
Whether you have just embarked on your spiritual journey or have been journeying for many years, I hope that you have recognized the importance of remembering spiritual milestones. It is important not only to remember these milestones, but also to share them with others.

During our study of Joshua, we have learned about God's protection, His promises, and His principles that assist us in our spiritual journey, as they did the Israelites. We have seen God's hand at work in memorable ways as He guided the Israelites from slavery in Egypt to claiming their inheritance of the Promised Land. Throughout their journey, they established different memorials that they continued to share with each other and with their children. We, too, need to share with others what wonderful works God has accomplished in our lives.

What stood out to you as you read the Key Box?

Read the scriptures below. When answering the questions, reflect on the theme of this section: *Remembering Our Spiritual Milestones*. When you write your answers, ask yourself how this applies to your life or your life experiences.

Be prepared to share what the Lord has been and is doing in your life as you have studied the book of Joshua.

Note several of the promises you have learned through the study.

List some of the principles you have discovered as you studied Joshua.

III. Continuing Our Spiritual Journey
- Dave Five and Day Six
- Key Passage: Philippians 2:12

Read the Key Passage and write down your personal insights.

_____
_____
_____
_____

> **Key Box**
> Like Joshua, I challenge you to *choose for yourselves this day whom you will serve*. Then, move forward in your spiritual journey through drawing near to God on a daily basis. As we studied Joshua, the Life Applications in each lesson have suggested different ways that will assist you in your journey. I challenge you to make the choice that Ezekiel 18:31 describes, *Cast away from you all the transgressions which you have committed, and get yourselves a new heart and a new spirit.*

What stood out to you as you read the Key Box?

_____
_____
_____
_____

Read the scriptures below. When answering the questions, reflect on the theme of this section: *Continuing Our Spiritual Journey*. When you write your answers, ask yourself how this applies to your life or your life experiences.

Describe practical ways that you can walk out these promises and principles in your spiritual journey.

_____
_____

How does reading God's Word daily and sharing your insights with a friend help you in your spiritual journey?

Life Applications
- Commit your life anew to the Lord and surrender afresh to His plans.
- Continue to study God's Word.
- Ask and allow the Holy Spirit to deepen your understanding of God's Word.
- Pray for continued renewal of your love for God and for all that He wants to do in your life.

Prayer
Heavenly Father,

Help me to daily surrender to the work of Your Holy Spirit in me and to always remember Your faithfulness and the mighty things You have done in my life. Forgive me when I forget to thank You for Your undeserved grace and mercy.

In Jesus' Name,
Amen

Notes

BIBLIOGRAPHY

Baker, Kenneth, General Editor. *The NIV Study Bible*. Grand Rapids, MI: Zondervan Publishing House.

Henry, Matthew. *Matthew Henry's Commentary*. Grand Rapids, MI: Zondervan Publishing House. 1960.

Getz, Gene A. *Joshua Living as a Consistent Role Model*. Nashville, TN. Broadman & Holman Publishers, 1995.

Hayford, Jack W. *Possessing the Promise of God: A Study of Joshua & Judges* Nashville, TN: Thomas Nelson Publishers, 1997

Huffman, John. *Mastering the Old Testament: Joshua*. Nashville, TN: Word Publishing, 1986.

Keller, W. Phillip. *Joshua: Mighty Warrior and Man of Faith.* Grand Rapids, MI: Kregel Publications, 1992.

Kent, Dan G. *Layman's Bible Book Commentary: Joshua Judges, Ruth Vol. 4*. Nashville, TN: Broadman Press, 1980

Peterson, Eugene. *The Message*. Colorado Springs, CO: NavPress. 2002.

Stedman, Ray. *Joshua Guidebook to Victory*. Internet Reference from pbc.org. Pala Alto, CA: Discovery Publishing. 1995

Strong James. *Strong's Exhaustive Concordance of the Bible*. Nashville, TN: World Bible Publisher, 1986.

Vine, W.E., Merril F. Unger, and William White. *Vines Expository of Biblical Words*. Nashville, TN: Thomas Nelson Publishers. 1985.

Wiersbe, Warren W. *Be Strong*. Colorado Springs, CO: Chariot Victor Publishing, 1993.

Zodhiates, Spiros. *The Hebrew-Greek Key Study Bible*. Chattanooga, TN: AMG Publishers 1984.

Made in the USA
Columbia, SC
19 January 2023